Women in Charge

By Leslie Dinaberg

The Child's World®

www.childsworld.com

Published in the United States of America by The Child's World®
1980 Lookout Drive • Mankato, MN 56003-1705
800-599-READ • www.childsworld.com

ACKNOWLEDGMENTS

The Child's World® : Mary Berendes, Publishing Director

Produced by Shoreline Publishing Group LLC
President / Editorial Director: James Buckley, Jr.
Designer: Tom Carling, carlingdesign.com
Cover Design: Slimfilms

Photo Credits
Cover–Corbis (4).
Interior–AP/Wide World: 3, 11, 15, 20, 22; Corbis: 5, 8, 12, 16, 17, 1,
24, 27, 28; Library of Congress: 6, 7, 9

LIBRARY OF CONGRESS CATALOG-IN-PUBLICATION DATA

Dinaberg, Leslie.
  Women in charge / by Leslie Dinaberg.
    p. cm. — (Reading rocks!)
  Includes index.
  ISBN-13: 978-1-59296-870-1 (library bound : alk. paper)
  ISBN-10: 1-59296-870-8 (library bound : alk. paper)
 1. Women—History. 2. Women politicians. 3. Businesswomen. I.
Title. II. Series.

HQ1121.D56 2007
305.4209—dc22

                                    2007004196

CONTENTS

WOMEN IN History

Women have been shaping the ways of the world since time began. But it would be hard to find them in history books until the last century. Men made almost all the decisions and held all the important jobs. Women were not allowed to do very much. In most places, they couldn't even vote to choose their leaders. However, some women became very important leaders themselves.

Cleopatra of Egypt was one of the most powerful women in history. When she was just 17 years

This sculpture shows how Cleopatra might have looked. It shows the style of clothing in ancient Egypt.

old, she became queen and ruled as Egypt's last **pharaoh** between 51 and 30 B.C. Cleopatra had to battle her brother, Ptolemy (TOL-uh-mee), for control. Cleopatra won, with the help of Julius Caesar. He was a Roman emperor who fell in love with her.

Ancient Egyptians called their leaders "pharaohs" (FARE-ohz). Pharaohs were treated like gods.

Eleanor Roosevelt (left) met with many American leaders, such as New York mayor Fiorello LaGuardia.

Closer to our own time, Eleanor Roosevelt had more effect on American life than any other woman in U.S. history. She was the wife of President Franklin Delano Roosevelt (he was President from 1932 to 1944). From that position of **influence**, Eleanor spoke out for women's rights, the rights of Native Americans, the homeless, and **minorities**. She also wrote a newspaper column called "My Day" from 1936 to 1962. The column brought her views to millions of Americans.

In the 1930s, Eleanor showed Americans how they could help others by working in this soup kitchen.

Eleanor also represented the U.S. worldwide at the United Nations. There she helped write the Universal Declaration of Human Rights. Eleanor was so respected that she was known as the "First Lady of the World." One of the sayings she lived by was, "Do what you feel in your heart to be right."

A pacifist is a person who is against all forms of violence, especially war.

America was almost 150 years old before women joined the national government. In 1916, Jeannette Rankin of Montana was the first woman to serve in the U.S. Congress. She was a **pacifist**. She was one of the few people in government to vote against the U.S. entering World Wars I and II.

Rosa Parks

Rosa Parks didn't set out to become a rebel, but she became known as the woman who changed a nation. After work one night in Montgomery, Alabama, in 1955, she boarded a bus for home. Rosa, an African-American woman, was ordered to give up her seat for a white passenger. She refused to give up her seat. That simple act of protest sparked the civil-rights movement and eventually led to the end of **segregation**.

Jeannette Rankin spoke out against war from her place in Congress.

Geraldine Ferraro earned a place in history as the first woman vice-presidential **candidate**. She ran as a Democrat in 1984, alongside Walter Mondale.

The first woman to serve as a U.S. senator was Rebecca Felton of Georgia. She was appointed to the job in 1922, and served for two days.

The first woman elected as a senator was Hattie Wyatt Caraway of Arkansas. In 1932, she was elected for a full **term**, and reelected in 1938.

In modern times, few women have had as much power as Golda Meir. She was the **prime minister** of Israel from 1969–1974. She was also one of the 24 signers of the document that created Israel, similar to the United States' Declaration of Independence.

The modern nation of Israel was created in 1948, following World War II.

She was born in Ukraine as Golda Mabovitz, and later changed her name to Meir, which means "makes a light" in Hebrew. As a child, her mother's nickname for her was *kochleffl* (kock-LEFF-ful, which means "stirring spoon"), because she was always stirring things up. After living briefly in the United States, she and her family moved to what would be Israel in 1921.

Golda became one of the world's most famous grandmothers when she took office in 1969—she was 71 years old. Under her leadership, the country went to war with Egypt and Syria. She served until 1974.

Meir met with many world leaders, including U.S. President Richard Nixon.

POLITICAL Leaders

In the past century, women have made great progress in gaining places among the world's leaders. More than in any other time in history, women are playing important roles in the world. Many women have become leaders of large nations or hold important jobs in their governments.

For instance, in 2006, Angela Merkel became the **chancellor** of Germany. She is the first female leader of that country. She is a **physicist**. She has used her scientific way of looking at things to help fix Germany's health-care system and tax plans. She is also a strong friend to Americans and works hard to bring the countries together. In truly modern style, Angela usually talks with her staff by text messages from her cell phone.

Angela Merkel (left) walks with another female leader, South Korea's Prime Minister Han Myung Sook.

In 2005, Condoleezza Rice became the second female U.S. secretary of state. Madeleine Albright was the first and worked from 1997–2001. Today, Condoleezza is considered to be one of the most powerful women in the world. She helps President George W. Bush decide the best way to handle problems around

Here Comes The Judge

The United States Supreme Court justices are nine of the most powerful people in the world. Their decisions affect the lives of millions of Americans. In 1981, Sandra Day O'Connor was the first woman named to the Supreme Court. She **retired** in 2005. Ruth Bader Ginsburg (left) is the second woman on the United States Supreme Court, and she is still serving.

As secretary of state, Rice speaks for America to countries around the world.

the world. Rice travels more than a half a million miles each year, visiting dozens of countries. She might find herself in a half-dozen countries in a week! Condoleezza is also an excellent piano player and sometimes plays for foreign visitors.

Wu Yi uses her scientific knowledge to help China's government make decisions for the country.

Wu Yi is one of four **vice premiers** of China. She is known as an "iron lady" for her strong views and direct ways. Few women around the world are as important to their governments as Wu Yi. She is also the minister of health. Wu has a degree in petroleum engineering. She was also the deputy mayor of China's capital city, Beijing.

Being a queen is a more traditional way for women to have power. Queen Elizabeth II of the United Kingdom has served her nation since 1953. She has ruled longer than any other current female leader. Other queens currently ruling countries include Queen Margrethe II of Denmark and Queen Beatrix of the Netherlands.

Like most queens, Queen Elizabeth's role is more ceremonial. Elected leaders actually run the government for her.

Ireland has had two female presidents. Mary McAleese has been president since 1997. Mary Robinson was president before her. President McAleese has had her job longer than any other elected female leader.

Here, Mary McAleese meets with South African president Nelson Mandela.

When she was a little girl, Mary's family priest told her that she could not be a lawyer because she was a girl. Her mom got so angry, she pulled the chair out from under the priest. Then her mom screamed at the priest, "YOU...OUT!" She told Mary, "And you, IGNORE HIM!" Mary is a great example that you can do anything if you set your mind to it.

While America has yet to have its first female president, Nancy Pelosi became the first female Speaker of the House of Representatives in 2007. In this important position, Nancy directs the House members in planning which laws they will vote on.

If the U.S. president dies or leaves office, the vice president takes over. The Speaker of the House is then second in line, behind only the vice president.

WOMEN IN Business

Along with taking a bigger part in politics, women play important roles in business. Here's a look at some notable women in business.

Indra Nooyi is Pepsi's CEO (Chief Executive Officer—the top job in a company). The company is worth more than $100 billion!

Before moving to the top of the Pepsi company, Indra helped it make deals to buy other companies. She believes that the secret to business success is always being ready to change. "The minute you've developed a new way of doing business," she says. "it's [out of date], because somebody is going to copy it."

OPPOSITE PAGE
Pepsi CEO Indra Nooyi was born in India. In 2006, two important business magazines named her the most powerful woman in business.

In honor of her business success, Anne Mulcahy received a special honor from New York University.

Xerox (ZEER-ocks) surprised the business world in 2001 by naming Anne Mulcahy as its first woman CEO. Xerox is one of the largest companies in the world. It is best known for its copiers, but it also makes printers, scanners, and fax machines.

Anne may be the boss, but working at Xerox is a family affair. Her husband is retired from Xerox, and her older brother has an important job, too. On the day that her appointment to CEO was announced, the **value** of the company dropped 15 percent. "That was a real confidence builder," she joked.

The value of a company is created by how much its shares of stock, or pieces of ownership, are worth.

I Am the Boss of Me

Up until 1920, women in the United States weren't allowed to vote. Most states didn't even allow women to own property. Well, have girls ever come a long way! There are now more than 10 million female business owners nationwide. Some of the most famous were clothing design legend Coco Chanel; Ruth Handler, who invented the Barbie Doll; and Katharine Graham, who was the publisher and owner of the *Washington Post* newspaper.

Meg Whitman and eBay have helped millions of people make money by selling things online.

Another major business leader is Meg Whitman. She is in charge of eBay, the world's biggest online auction house. It's also one of the biggest Internet success stories.

Meg Whitman and eBay have helped millions of people make money by selling things online.

When Meg joined eBay, the company had 30 employees and only operated in the United States. The company now has offices around the world and more than 9,000 employees! Before joining eBay, Meg worked for the toy company Hasbro and was in charge of Playskool and Mr. Potato Head. Meg is now one of the richest women in the world.

Meg went to Princeton University. She has given that school a lot of money to help its students. She knows how important a good education was to her success. She wants to make sure that other students—both men and women—can follow in her footsteps.

It's nothing new to find women in entertainment. Today, women are a big part of the entertainment business—both in front of the cameras as well as behind them.

See if you can guess where Oprah got the name of Harpo, her television company. That's right— it's her first name spelled backward!

Perhaps the most successful woman in entertainment is Oprah Winfrey. The TV host from Chicago was the first African-American woman with her own TV company. She is also television's highest-paid entertainer. Oprah's talk show reaches more than 15 million people every day.

She works to end child abuse, and tells people about the importance of reading. She also gives generously to colleges and universities and other worthy causes.

Oprah is also an actress who was **nominated** for an Academy Award. She publishes her own magazine, too. Oprah proves what she tells young people: There is nothing you can't do if you try hard enough.

Oprah Winfrey is a success in many fields of business.

In 2005, Bill and Melinda Gates (in back row) met with women in India who were being helped by their charity work.

Besides politics and business, women play a huge role in helping people, too. Every year a disease called **malaria** kills 1 million people—most of them African children under the age of five. Scientists are closer to finding a cure thanks in large part to Melinda Gates. She works with her husband, Bill Gates, to provide money to experts working on a cure. Bill founded the computer company Microsoft and is the richest person in the world. Melinda helps run the Gates **Foundation**, which has more money than any other **charity**.

Melinda has a big job! She's also helping to find cures for AIDS and other diseases. Her good ideas and the foundation's money are helping with dozens of other health, education, and social problems.

Women have only been a big part of political and business leadership for a century or so. But they have come a long way in that time . . . now there is nothing that a woman can't do!

GLOSSARY

candidate   a person running for political office

chancellor   the title of the leader of Germany's government

charity   an organization that helps people in need

foundation   an organization set up to help run charities

influence   the ability to make an impact or create change in a situation

malaria   a blood disease caused by tiny creatures spread by mosquitoes

minorities   in a society, the members of smaller ethnic groups

nominated   chosen to be considered for an award

pacifist   a person who is against all forms of violence, especially war

pharaoh   a ruler of ancient Egypt

physicist   a scientist who studies matter and energy

prime minister   the title given to the leaders of some countries

retired   to stop working or to give up a job, often because of age

segregation   the forced separation of people based on their race

term   the length of time a person holds a political office

value   what something is worth

vice premier   a person who is second in line behind a premier, or ruler of a country

FIND OUT MORE

BOOKS

Cleopatra: The Queen of Kings
by Fiona MacDonald (DK Publishing, 2001)
A great book with lots of fascinating facts about the life of
Cleopatra.

Famous American Women
by Gregory Guiteras (Dover Publications, 2001)
A coloring book that spotlights the achievements of 45 famous
American women.

Oprah Winfrey: Television Star (Library of Famous Women)
by Steven Otfinoski (Blackbirch Press, 1994)
Read about the life and career of one of entertainment's most
successful women.

**The Usborne Book of Famous Women: From Nefertiti to
Thatcher (Famous Lives Series)**
by Richard Dungworth and Philippa Wingate (E.D.C.
Publishing, 1997)
A richly illustrated book of short biographies of famous
women.

WEB SITES

Visit our Web page for lots of links about women in important
positions around the world: www.childsworld.com/links

Note to Parents, Teachers, and Librarians: We routinely check our Web links to
make sure they're safe, active sites—so encourage your readers to check them out!

INDEX

LESLIE DINABERG has more than 15 years of experience as a writer and editor for a variety of magazines, Web sites, and newspapers. The former executive editor of *SAM Magazine* and the former managing editor of *Hispanic Business Magazine* and *SuperOnda Magazine*, she currently writes a weekly newspaper column called "South Coasting."